MONSTER RIDDLES

by Louis Phillips
pictures by Arlene Dubanevich
Viking

VIKING
Published by the Penguin Group
Penguin Putnam Inc., 375 Hudson Street, New York, New York 10014, U.S.A.
Penguin Books Ltd, 27 Wrights Lane, London W8 5TZ, England
Penguin Books Australia Ltd, Ringwood, Victoria, Australia
Penguin Books Canada Ltd, 10 Alcorn Avenue, Toronto, Ontario, Canada M4V 3B2
Penguin Books (N.Z.) Ltd, 182–190 Wairau Road, Auckland 10, New Zealand

Penguin Books Ltd, Registered Offices: Harmondsworth, Middlesex, England

First published in 1998 by Viking, a member of Penguin Putnam Inc.
Published simultaneously in Puffin Books

1 3 5 7 9 10 8 6 4 2

Text copyright © Louis Phillips, 1998
Illustrations copyright © Arlene Dubanevich, 1998
All rights reserved

LIBRARY OF CONGRESS CATALOGING-IN-PUBLICATION DATA
Phillips, Louis.
Monster riddles / by Louis Phillips ;
illustrated by Arlene Dubanevich.
p. cm. — (A Viking easy-to-read)
Summary: A collection of riddles about monsters,
vampires, ghosts, and other creatures.
ISBN 0-670-87459-0 (hardcover).—ISBN 0-14-038790-0 (pbk.)
1. Riddles, Juvenile. 2. Monsters—Juvenile humor.
[1. Monsters—Wit and humor. 2. Riddles. 3. Jokes.]
I. Dubanevich, Arlene, illus. II. Title. III. Series
PN6371.5.P497 1998 818'.5402—dc21 96-47722 CIP AC

Printed in USA
Set in New Century Schoolbook

Viking® and Easy-to-Read® are registered trademarks of
Penguin Books USA Inc.

Reading level 2.3

To Barbara, Marvin, and
Matthew Wasserman
—L. P.

For Chloe, who always answers
with a riddle
—A. D.

What do you get if you cross
Godzilla with peanut butter?

A monster that sticks
to the roof of your mouth.

A monster goes to a restaurant.
What does he eat?

The building.

How does a monster count to 23?

On her fingers.

Who won the first prize in the monsters' beauty contest?

Nobody!

What do you get when you cross
Dracula with a parrot?

A bird that says, "Polly wants your neck!"

Why does Count Dracula drink blood?

Orange juice costs too much.

Why does Count Dracula drink blood?

So he won't have to
recycle the empty bottles.

Why was Dracula's big sister mad at Dracula?

He was a pain in the neck.

What is white, covered with bandages, and goes putt, putt, putt?

A mummy wearing an outboard motor.

Why is the mummy so forgetful?

Because she is wrapped up in her work.

Where does a 3,000-pound
monster sleep?

Anyplace it wants to.

What do you call monsters who eat their parents for lunch?

Orphans.

How did the giant snake feel
about the pretty girl next door?

He had a crush on her.

What is 9 feet long, has 6 legs, and would kill you if it fell out of a tree?

A pool table.

What is the ghost's favorite ride at the fair?

The roller ghoster.

What is the favorite baseball
team of all ghosts?

The Toronto Boo Jays.

What kind of pants do ghosts
wear?

Boo jeans.

What is brown on the outside and hairy on the inside?

A werewolf in a paper bag.

What do you get when you cross bread with a werewolf?

A sandwich that gets hairy under a full moon.

Why did the werewolf stare at the hairbrush?

He thought it was a mirror.

What goes ha ha, ha ha, ha ha, clunk?

A monster laughing its head off.

Why did the giant ape climb to the top of the Empire State Building?

Because she couldn't fit into the elevator.

What do you get if you cross a
man-eating shark with a parrot?

A monster that talks your ear off.

What is a monster's favorite food in summer?

Ice scream.

What is a monster's favorite bed-time story?

Sleeping Ugly.

Where does Dracula keep his life savings?

In a blood bank.

Who is Dracula's favorite
television and movie character?

Batman, of course.

How do you make a vampire
float?

You mix two scoops of ice cream,
a glass of soda, and a vampire.

What do you call a monster who is twelve feet tall?

Shorty.

What do you call a monster with half a brain?

The smartest monster on the block.

Why don't zombies make good dancers?

Because they are dead on their feet.

Why was the skeleton so unhappy at the party?

He had no body to dance with.

What did the sheet say to the ghost?

"Hold still. I've got you covered!"

What did one ghost say to the other?

"Do you believe in people?"

What happened when the giant joined the circus?

She stole the show.

What do you get if you cross a skunk with a 90-foot giant?

I don't know, but whatever it is, it stinks to high heaven.

Why did Dracula return his
electric toothbrush?

Because he didn't have any electric teeth.

What does Dracula bring to a baseball game?

He brings the bats, of course.

What is the best thing to put on a vampire's coffin?

A very tight lid.

What is brown on the outside, green on the inside, and has fins?

A chocolate-covered swamp monster.

Why does the two-headed monster forget everything he hears?

It goes in one ear and out the other ear and in the other ear and out the other ear.

What do you say to a two-headed monster?

"Hi. Hi."